CHAPTER 1

INTRODUCTION

> Military subordination to civilian policymakers is a recurring and sensitive issue in civil-military relations within the United States. The political leadership and the American people expect their military to execute the guidance provided by elected officials faithfully. Yet, the American people also demand that their military perform professionally and win the nation's wars.
> — Harry R. Yarger, *Strategic Theory for the 21st Century*

The subordinate role of military professionals to civilian policy makers is an on-going narrative in the American experience that is yet to be fully resolved because of the complex issues that govern strategic policy formulation and design. In the history of the United States, there were episodic tensions that prompted significant changes in civil-military relations. Some of these changes have profound impact on how we formulate and implement national strategic policies. From the founding of the nation, to the firing of General Stanley McChrystal as commander of International Security Assistance Force in Afghanistan in June 2010, and to the more recent forced retirement in March 2013 of Marine General James Mattis as U.S. Central Command Commander (Halper 2013; Lee 2013),[1] there are numerous examples in U.S. history on the struggle for proper civil-military relations.

The American people and its elected leaders expect their military professionals to faithfully execute their given mission without reservations. But, the view that military professionals will become "yes men" with every policy decision made by civilian policy makers sometimes generates tension in civil-military relations, because it may imply

---

[1]Multiple reports from different media outlets points to disagreement with the Obama administration on Iran led to General James Mattis forced retirement.

2006. These three case studies were selected using the following criteria: (1) availability of research materials, (2) type of the ethical dilemmas they presented (3) level (i.e., strategic) of military professionals and civilian policy makers, (4) the period they occurred, and (5) the type and context where friction points or tensions occur between strategic civilian policy makers and military professionals (i.e., Commander in Chief versus a Field Commander in President Truman versus General MacArthur; Commander in Chief versus Service Chiefs in President Eisenhower versus Generals; and Secretary of Defense versus Field Commanders in Generals' Revolt of 2006).

This study also addresses the following secondary questions: (1) When faced with a policy or plan that they do not support, what may be the proper course of action for military professionals? (2) What are the ethical dilemmas of following orders that are inconsistent with proper military strategy? (3) When is it appropriate for military professionals to voice their opinion or raise their objections? And (4) is there an appropriate venue for military professionals to voice their opinion or raise their objections?

This study only focuses on the U.S. Army. It is not the intent or purview of this study to analyze the civilian policy makers because of the significant difference in constraints between military professionals and civilian policy makers.[3] The goals of this study are that the conclusions derived will contribute to the enhancement of civil-military relations; add to the body of knowledge on the subject; inspire further analysis of the underlying issues; and facilitate discussion on the subject to generate meaningful

_____

[3]Military professionals are expected to be both non partisan and apolitical when providing military advice to civilian policy makers.

4

solutions that enhances civil-military relations for the better. Breakdowns in U.S. civil-military relations create animosity between civilian policy makers and military professionals. Such animosity can breed resentment that often results in partisanship. Partisanship can doom the process of creating sound policies and effective strategies in pursuing critical U.S. national interest.

The intended audiences of this study are the following: military professionals, federal elected officials, federal agency or department heads, researchers, academics, teachers, and students of civil-military relations. Less than 22 percent of all current elected officials in Congress and only three cabinet members of the Obama administration have military backgrounds (Manning 2012, 7). Consequently, this may result in a lack of understanding by elected officials of why, what, and who constitutes the present military professionals, their background, training, and level of experience that sums up their professional credentials. The aim is that the individuals identified above will find the study helpful in understanding military professionals and the friction points in civil-military relations to develop an understanding of the ethical dilemmas faced by military professionals.

This study uses the following key terms.

Army ethic: The collection of values, beliefs, ideals, and principles held by the Army profession and embedded in its culture (CAPE 2012).

Army professional: A member of the Army profession who meets the Army's professional certification criteria of competence, character, and commitment (CAPE 2012).

Army profession: A unique vocation of experts certified in the design, generation, support, and ethical application of land power, serving under civilian authority and entrusted to defend the Constitution and the rights and interests of the American people (CAPE 2012).

Civilian policy makers: Elected and, or, appointed civilian heads of the U.S. government.

Ethics: A form of philosophy that deals with principles and concepts that guide right and wrong behavior (Mattox 2012).

Ethos: The indispensible but intangible motivating spirit of Army professionals' committed to the Army Ethic (CAPE 2012).

Generals: In President Eisenhower versus the Generals, Generals refer to Generals Mathew B. Ridgeway and Maxwell D. Taylor, former 19th and 20th Army Chief of Staff respectively.

Generals: In the Generals' Revolt of 2006, Generals refer to retired Major General Paul D. Eaton, Major General John R.S. Batiste, Major General John M. Riggs, and Major General Charles Swannack.

Government officials: In this study refers to members of Congress and federal agency or department heads.

Leadership: The process of influencing people by providing purpose, direction, and motivation while operating to accomplish the mission and improving the organization (Department of the Army 2012, 1).

Members of the civil-military relations spectrum: This refers to the executive, legislative, and military members of the U.S. government.

Military dissent: In this study is defined as the expressed disagreement between military professionals and civilian policy makers over policies or strategies based on their judgment.

Military professionals: Defined here as strategic leaders in the U.S. Army, primarily General Officers from one to four stars in rank.

Morals: Describes personal behaviors of right and wrong (Mattox 2012).

Moral courage: The capacity to overcome the fear of shame and humiliation in order to admit one's mistakes, to confess a wrong, to reject evil conformity, to denounce injustice, and to defy immoral or imprudent orders (Miller 2000, 254).

Professional military judgment: In this study refers to the decisions made by military professionals based on their training, experience, and level of expertise.

Professional soldier: An expert, a volunteer certified in the Profession of Arms, bonded with comrades in a shared identify and culture of sacrifice and service to the Nation and the Constitution, who adheres to the Army Ethic and is a steward of the future of the profession (CAPE 2012).

This chapter provided the context for the research question, illustrated its significance, and outlined the other questions that will be answered through the course of this study. The next chapter discusses the available and relevant literature on the topic that answers the research questions. Chapter 2, the literature review, presents the different theories of civil-military relations, examines the different significant events over the years that brought tensions in civil-military relations at the forefront of the national conversation, and reviews contemporary writings on ethics in U.S. civil-military relations.

CHAPTER 2

LITERATURE REVIEW

> Nor indeed is it sensible to summon soldiers, as many governments do when they are planning a war, and ask them for purely military advice. . . . Only if statesman look to certain military moves and actions to produce effects that are foreign to their nature do political decisions influence operations for the worse.
>
> — Carl von Clausewitz, *On War*

The previous chapter provided the context for this study. This chapter reviews the significant literature used in this study. It focuses on three major areas: different theories in civil-military relations, the three case studies, and contemporary writings on military ethics. The purpose of this chapter is to provide a working framework for examining the different theories and significant writing to illustrate their relevance in answering the research questions.

Different Theories in Civil-Military Relations

The contemporary study of theories in civil-military relations in the United States begins with Samuel P. Huntington's influential work *The Soldier and the State: The Theory and Politics of Civil-Military Relations* published in 1957. Huntington's work centers on the theory of subjective versus objective civilian control over the military. In defining his premise for subjective control, Huntington emphasizes the primacy of civilian authority over the military (Huntington 1957, 80). In Huntington's view, subjective control provides the indispensable oversight of the military. Huntington's outlook on objective control centers on the professionalization of the military officers corps. Objective control seems to imply autonomy based on distinctive professional framework. Huntington's distinct professional framework is based on professional

8

"expertise, responsibility, and corporateness" within the military officer corps (Huntington 1957, 7-11).

Huntington's theory in civil-military relations is followed by Morris Janowitz's, *The Professional Soldier: A Social and Political Portrait* published in 1960. Janowitz's theory on civil-military relations is based on the concept of a constabulary force[4] evolving from the citizen-soldier conscription or system (Janowitz 1960, 422). Janowitz's view on civil-military relations is based on his observations of the impact of new technology on the military and the residual changes it produces. Janowitz contends that these changes make the military adopt a more civilian outlook, but it does not necessarily result in making civilians adopt a militarized attitude (Janowitz 1960, 31). Janowitz illustrates the need for the military to stay outside of the political arena, but is cognizant of the challenges this poses because "in the United States, where political leadership is diffused, civilian politicians have come to assume that the military will be an active ingredient in decision-making about national security" (Janowitz 1964, 342).

Subsequent to the work of Huntington and Janowitz is the concordance theory developed by Rebecca L. Schiff. Her theory first came to light in her article "Civil-military Relations Reconsidered: A Theory of Concordance" published in 1995 by *Armed Forces and Society* and expounded on in her book *The Military and Domestic Politics: A Concordance Theory of Civil-Military Relations* published in 2009. According to Schiff, the prevailing theory of separation between civilian and military establishment when it

---

[4]A military constabulary force is an institution that is continuously prepared to act, committed to the minimum use of force, and seeks viable international relations, rather than victory. The constabulary force concept covers the entire range of military operations, capabilities, and organizations.

comes to domestic intervention by the military should be re-examined. She argues that the "three partners–the military, the political elites, and the citizenry should aim for a cooperative relationship that may or may not entail the separation of political and military institutions" (Schiff 1995, 32). As a theory, concordance provides both descriptive and prescriptive approaches and does not limit itself to one civil-military scenario. It explains the institutional and cultural conditions that affect the distinctive relationships among the three partners (Schiff 1995, 47). It also envisions that if these partners agree on the "four indicators-the social composition of the officer corps, the political decision-making process, recruitment method, and military style, then military intervention in domestic affairs is less likely to occur" (Schiff 1995, 44).

In the more recent period, Eliot A. Cohen's work *Supreme Command: Soldiers, Statesmen, and Leadership in Wartime* published in 2002 hypothesized the "unequal dialogue" between civilian policy makers and military professionals. By unequal dialogue, Cohen posits that the communicative exchange between military leaders and civilian policy makers must be sincere, truthful, and sometimes combative, but always unequal with deference to civilian policy makers (Cohen 2002, 209). Because ultimately, "a politician finds himself managing military alliances, deciding the nature of acceptable risk, shaping operational choices, and reconstructing military organizations," civilian policy makers must therefore have the final say on the conduct and execution of policies and strategy (Cohen 2002, 10). Cohen makes the assertion that unequal dialogue is essential in maintaining the proper context for communication between military leaders and civilian policy makers. According to Cohen, the job of military leaders is to execute military plans to achieve political objectives, not the other way around, but more so because military leaders are limited by their training and experiences (2002, 233).

The last of the theories reviewed in this study is the principal-agent theory from Peter D. Feaver's work *Armed Servants: Agency, Oversight, and Civil-Military Relations* published in 2003. Feaver's principal-agent theory focuses on the significance of delegation and monitoring mechanisms employed by civilian policy makers to determine whether military leaders are working or shirking from their responsibility. The principal-agent theory provides context for understanding civilian control over the military (Feaver 2003, 56). Feaver's work is significant in understanding the motivation for how civilian policy makers and military professionals interact and execute their mandate in a democratic society.

Other theorists of civil-military relations worthy of consideration but who do not rise to the level of deliberation in this study are: (1) Peter Roman and David Tarr's process approach in their work "The Joint Chiefs of Staff: From Service Parochialism to Jointness" published in 1998. The process approach focuses mainly on the evolving role of the Joint Chiefs of Staff (JCS) in the post-Goldwater-Nichols period. It illustrates the impact of the American political process in politicizing the military by drawing the military leadership into active participation in the political functions of government. This theory does not offer methods in deciphering civil-military relations like the previous five theories. (2) Michael C. Desch's functional approach from his work *Civilian Control of the Military: The Changing Security Environment* published in 2001. The functional approach provides rationale to the perception that civilian authorities have not been able to exert greater control over military policies and decision making. As a theory it does not present an approach dealing with the proper roles of military professionals and civilian policy makers. (3) Deborah Avant's privatization model in her work "The Privatization of Security and Change in the Control of Force" published in 2004. Privatization examines the private sector incursion into public policy is in the realm of national security. It does not address any of the issues dealing with separation of roles, duties, and responsibilities between military professionals and civilian policy makers. (5) Dale Herspring's relationship principle in his work *The Pentagon and the Presidency: Civil-Military Relations from FDR to George W. Bush* published in 2005. Herspring's theory explains civil-military relations in terms of differences in culture between military professionals and civilian policy makers. Herspring's theory focuses on civil-military relations at the micro-level of the conflict between military professionals and civilian policy makers.

These five additional theories provide a broader context for understanding civil-military relations and they were reviewed during the course of this study. The information gleaned from these theories does not rise to the level of significance in this study, but students of civil-military relations can profit from reviewing them. They provide additional perspective and rationale in civil-military relations that may be helpful to students in deciphering the complex relationship between members of the civil military spectrum.

Although, the five main theories reviewed in this study provide a framework for understanding the issues, they do not present clear solutions or delineations on the proper roles of civilian policy makers and military professionals in the formulation and implementation of policies and strategies. Due to the lack of congruence, gaps, and flaws among the different theories, there is no clear path or road map for establishing or evaluating the proper roles of civilian policy makers and military professionals when designing and implementing national strategic policies. As a consequence, the current theories or models in civil-military relations neither address nor provide a working framework for resolving ethical dilemmas that arise when there is a conflict between formulating and implementing policies and strategies to achieve U.S. national interests between military professionals and their civilian superiors.

Literature on the Three Case Studies

There is significant scholarly work available when examining the topic of President Truman versus General MacArthur. Among these works is Michael D. Pearlman's *Truman and MacArthur: Policy, Politics, and the Hunger for Honor and Renown* published in 2008 and Richard H. Rovere with Arthur Schlesinger Jr. in *General MacArthur and President Truman: The Struggle for Control of American Foreign Policy* published in 1992. These books illustrate the consensus among noted scholars, authors, and writers on the subject that General MacArthur overstepped his bounds in publicly expressing his disagreement with President Truman's U.S. foreign policy in Korea. John W. Spanier in "The Truman-MacArthur Controversy and the Korean War" published in 1959 among others, views General MacArthur's action of arguing his case in the media as a direct challenge to the civilian control of the military. Mel Gurtov's "From Korea to Vietnam: The Origins and Mindset of Postwar U.S. Interventionism" published in 2010 provides context to the U.S. strategic and policy mindset that led to the American involvement on those conflicts. Spencer C. Tucker's *The Korean War, 1950-53: From*

Maneuver to Stalemate published in 2010 on the occasion of the 60th anniversary of the Korean War provides an analytical account of the origin, impact, and outcome of the war.

Academic study on the topic from the U.S. military's institutions of higher learning like Lieutenant Colonel Allen R. Potter's thesis "The Truman–MacArthur Controversy: A Study in Political-Military Relations" completed in 1972 at the U.S. Army Command and General Staff College at Fort Leavenworth, Kansas came to some of the same conclusions but provides insight into the contrasting personality and strategic vision of President Truman and General MacArthur which contributed to the debacle. Other studies like Lieutenant Colonel Stephen A. Danner's "The Truman-Macarthur Tug of War–A Lingering Aftermath?" completed in 1993 at the U.S. Air Force Air War College at Maxwell AFB, Alabama looked into the impact of the incident by studying four cases of civil-military conflict: (1) General Mathew Ridgeway, U.S. Army Chief of Staff and Secretary of Defense Charles E. Wilson, (2) General William Westmoreland, the Joint Chiefs, and President Lyndon Johnson, (3) Major General John K. Singlaub, U.S. military chief of staff Korea and President Jimmy Carter, and (4) General Colin Powell, chairman JCS and President William J. Clinton. His conclusion is "that MacArthur's relief has not had an adverse restraining effect on civil-military relations when leaders of character and strength of will are involved" (Danner 1993, 23).

There is general affirmation among scholars, authors, and writers on the subject that General MacArthur violated one of the fundamental principles in civil-military relations by his political partisan actions in siding with or supporting Republican members of Congress against President Truman. Most authors on the subject agree that President Truman's action to relieve General MacArthur was the right thing to do, but

14

they do not fully examine the true motives behind General MacArthur's actions. The battle of wills between the two men irrevocably damaged the relationship which inevitably led to the abrupt firing of General MacArthur in 1951.

Analysis of scholastic work on President Eisenhower versus the Generals suggests that the disagreement between the President and the Generals was not on the President's leadership and authority, but with the assertion by the President that senior Army officers had no reservations on the strategy and force level structure proposition under the "New Look" policy. Many of the scholars, especially from the Army's own institutions of learning like Dr. Donald A. Carter, military Professor at West Point, in his article "Eisenhower versus the Generals" published in 2007 and Dr. Steven Metz Professor at the U.S. Army War College in his writing *Eisenhower as Strategist: The Coherent use of Military Power in War and Peace* published in 1993 concludes that the Generals' objection to President Eisenhower focused on two fundamental issues: first, conflict with the Soviet Union will not lead to a nuclear exchange and second, the proposed cuts to the Army threaten its ability to perform its missions. Prominent scholars working on the subject such as historian John Lewis Gaddis in *Strategies of Containment: A Critical Appraisal of Postwar American National Security Policy* published in 2005 and renowned lecturer Campbell Craig in *Destroying the Village: Eisenhower and Thermonuclear War* published in 1998 studied the New Look policy for its influence on the global events and ability to restrain and prevent nuclear war with the Soviet Union.

Andrew J. Bacevich, who wrote *The Pentomic Era: the U.S. Army Between Korea and Vietnam* published in 1986, was one of the few authors in that era who attempted to explain the Army's effort to fit within President Eisenhower's plan for the military. A subsequent writing, "The Paradox of Professionalism: Eisenhower, Ridgeway, and the Challenge to Civilian Control 1953-1955" published in 1997, was the closest writing that examined the disagreement between President Eisenhower and senior Army officers. Most of the writings on the Army's point of view at the time come from the memoirs and literary works of former Generals Maxwell D. Taylor's in *The Uncertain Trumpet* published in 1960 and *Swords and Plowshares* published in 1972, James Gavin's *War and Peace in the Space Age,* published in 1958, and Matthew Ridgeway as told to Harold H. Martin *Soldier: The Memoirs of Matthew Ridgeway* published in 1956.

On the Generals' Revolt of 2006, the majority of the literature centers on the consensus that the main key points of the Generals arguments were Secretary of Defense Donald H. Rumsfeld's: (1) mismanagement of the war, (2) failure to listen or accept the advice of military commanders, (3) apparent disregard for the consequences of implementing a flawed strategy in prosecuting the war and, (4) complicating the U.S. mission by alienating North Atlantic Treaty Organization allies. There is anecdotal mention of the incident in some of the biographies and autobiographies of the individuals involved and works on the period, like Secretary of Defense Donald H. Rumsfeld's *Known and Unknown: A Memoir* published in 2012, Thomas E. Ricks *Fiasco: The American Military Adventure in Iraq, 2003 to 2005* published in 2007, and Ambassador Lewis P. Bremer III with Author Malcolm McConnell *My Year in Iraq: The Struggle to Build a Future of hope* published in 2006. Bob Woodward's work *Plan of Attack,* published in 2004, chronicles President George W. Bush's administration wrestling with the issues of invading Iraq.

A great deal of the scholarly work on the subject of the Generals' Revolt of 2006 comes from the military's own institutional leader development programs. Writers and authors from the military's learning institutions who have written about the subject like Dr. Mackubin T. Owens, Professor of Strategy and Force Planning for the Naval War College in "Rumsfeld, the Generals, and the State of U.S. Civil-Military Relations" published in 2007, and Dr. Don M. Snider, Senior Fellow in the Center for the Army Profession and Ethic in "Dissent and Strategic Leadership of the Military Professions" published in 2008 do not squarely put all the blame on Secretary Rumsfeld's shoulders. The authors place equal blame for the military's failure to voice their dissatisfaction in an effective and coherent manner. Secretary Rumsfeld may have had an abrasive personality, but it was hardly enough reason to justify military dissent. Not liking your superior because of his personality seems shallow and does not merit justification for wanting him fired. Lieutenant Colonel Paul Yingling's article "A Failure in Generalship" published in 2007 was a scathing rebuke of failures in generalship in Iraq. His article highlights the failures of Army generals to prepare the Army for the Iraq War and Congress' abdication of its duty. Other writers, like Colonel Lewis R. Snyder in his U.S. Army War College program research project work "The Generals' Revolt and Civil-Military Relations" published in 2009 believed that the Generals' revolt was precipitated by Secretary Rumsfeld's refusal to acknowledge the experience and knowledge of key strategic leaders; and stubbornness to accept or even listen to divergent opinion. Snyder also believes that the gradual and continual politicization of the military along with a decline in military professionalism and ethical decision-making of the Generals contributed to setting the conditions for the revolt (2009, 1).

Study of available literature on the three case studies reveals a general consensus of pervading thoughts on the subjects by authors, writers, and scholars. Regarding the case of General MacArthur versus President Truman, the available literature illustrates the role of the United States in the Korean War and the public disagreement between General MacArthur and President Truman. Most of the writing about the topic focuses on the origins of the conflict, the roles of China, the United States, North and South Korea, and the actions of General MacArthur during the war. There is common accord among authors that General MacArthur's public dissent is one of the most significant challenges to civilian control of the military. But, they fail to consider the ethical dilemma that General MacArthur faced in following orders which were contrary to his best military judgment. The available literature does not address the ethical dilemma faced by General MacArthur.

In Eisenhower versus the Generals, most of the writings by academics and researchers on the subject explored the New Look policy as a strictly strategic foreign policy position and very few looked at the impact of the strategy on the military, particularly the U.S. Army who saw it as a direct threat to its existence. The contrasting views between President Eisenhower and the Generals in terms of the impact of the New Look policy on the Army are not fully examined. The available literature mainly focuses on the New Look policy as a strategic vision by the Eisenhower administration. The available literature does not address the appropriate actions available to military professionals when faced with the ethical dilemma of defending institutional survival.

Although, there are differing opinions on whose fault caused the Generals' Revolt of 2006, it is irrelevant to the consequences and impact of the act itself. Because the event was fairly recent, the available literature does not fully address many of the larger questions on the issues which brought about the conflict between Secretary Rumsfeld and the Generals. The questions of whether retired military professionals represent their former colleagues in their retirement, the role military commanders played in key decision making, the long term impact of the event are not answered by contemporary work on the subject. The available literature also does not explore the available options open to military professionals to voice their opinions when faced with ethical dilemmas.

<u>Contemporary Writings on Ethics in Civil-Military Relations</u>

Among the most contemporary work on civil-military relations comes from former *New York Times* reporter Thomas E. Ricks' *The Generals: American Military Command from World War II to today* published in 2012 which highlights the significant change in civil-military relations from World War II to present day. Ricks makes the comparison of the relationship between General George C. Marshall and President Franklin D. Roosevelt to today's generals and recent Commanders in Chief. Ricks makes the clear distinction that today's generals are more inclined to develop personal relationships or at least show propensity to develop a personal relationship with their civilian superiors which leads to perceived deference to them in matters of national security (Ricks 2012, 31). According to Ricks, this arrangement puts pliable men in the military hierarchy who have the propensity to go along with their civilian superiors and robs the nation of objective military advice (2012, 452). This relationship is dangerous at best; and the relationship that General Marshall had with President Eisenhower is probably the best model to emulate because it provides distance and prevents familiarity (Ricks 2012, 453).

In *Military Ethics and Virtues: An Interdisciplinary Approach for the 21st century* published in 2011, Professor Peter Olsthoorn seeks to provide an approach towards understanding traditional military virtues as they apply to the twenty-first century. Although his work primarily focuses on traditional military virtues, it also delves into the evolution of a new Western way of war. With the collapse of the Soviet Union, the core task for most militaries in the West changed from major conflict, to the conventional task of national defense (Olsthoorn 2011, 2). In the study, Professor Olsthoorn discusses the new constraints imposed on soldiers to behave more humanely and morally during conflicts and the subsequent effects this places on them. In his work Professor Olsthoorn, compares and contrasts the behaviors of conventional forces to their contemporary non-conventional adversaries. Professor Olsthoorn also explores the impact of the contemporary values of the society at large on the military's moral fabric.

Lieutenant Colonel Douglas W. Bennett's monograph "Military Advice and Civil-Military Relations" published in 2010 examines variables which impact the civil-military relationship with regards to understanding how military advice is received by civilian leaders. He concludes that the lack of military experience by civilian leaders does not detract from their ability to understand and develop strategic security policies; and military expertise provided by military leaders largely depends on the type of conflict in which they have expertise. He also highlights service parochialism as a critical factor in influencing civilian leaders' receptiveness to military advice. Donald B. Connelly's *The Unequal Professional Dialogue: American Civil-Military Relations and the Professional Military Ethic* published in 2010 examines the different theoretical frameworks dealing with professional dialogue in civil-military relations. Connelly supports his analysis by using different theories in civil-military relations providing context for the different dialogues between civilian policy makers and military professionals.

In *American Civil-military Relations: The Soldier and the State in a New Era* edited by Suzanne C. Nielsen and Don M. Snider published in 2009 contains numerous works on different subjects pertaining to civil-military relations. Significant among them was Colonel Matthew Moten's chapter on General Eric Shinseki. General Shinseki, then serving as Chief of Staff of the Army, was severely censured by his senior civilian superiors in the Department of Defense for giving an honest answer about the situation of post invasion in Iraq to Senator Carl Levin of the Senate Armed Services Committee during his testimony. Secretary of Defense Donald Rumsfeld and Under Secretary of Defense Paul Wolfowitz later criticized General Shinseki's assertion that additional troops were needed to secure Iraq after major combat operations. Both believed that Americans would be welcomed with open arms in Iraq. The work provides a wide range of views on the different branches or topics dealing with civil-military relations.

Lieutenant Colonel Jason K. Dempsey's *Our Army: Soldiers, Politics, and American Civil-Military Relations* published in 2009 provides insight into the political and social leanings of U.S. Army officers and enlisted personnel. Dempsey's work emphasizes the importance of being apolitical by military personnel, while providing perceptive details on the intricacies of the political outlook of officers and enlisted personnel in the U.S. Army. Dempsey's work disproves numerous commonly held assumptions about Army officers and enlisted personnel. Dempsey's work demonstrates that while Army officers are likely to be more conservative and republican; enlisted soldier's political leanings are more representative of the American public's demographics. Contrary to popular belief, enlisted soldiers are less partisan and politically active than they perceived. Dempsey's book presents the behavior and mind-set of both officers and enlisted personnel in the U.S.

Dr. Martin L. Cook's work *The Moral Warrior: Ethics and Service in the U.S. Military* published in 2004 analyzes the topic of military service and military ethics. Cook tackles individual moral responsibilities and ethical issues inherent in the military profession and endeavor. Dr. Cook's work provides a good context for examining and understanding military actions and reactions. Dr. Cook posits that the changing operational environment contributes to personal strain and conflict within military personnel because they have to adapt to constantly shifting situation. The residual effect of varying conditions and adversary causes military personnel to re-evaluate their response, an option which is not easy or immediate at times.

Military Professionalism, the Military Ethics, and Officership in the 21st century published in 1999 by Dr. Don M. Snider, Major John A. Nagl, and Major Tony Pfaff, examined the components of military professionalism.[5] In their study, the authors address the conflicts in each of the military professional components. In addressing the conflict of the ethical component of military professionalism, the authors suggest that there is serious internal conflict between personal ethics and military ethics among Army officers. The authors believe that professional military ethics is being challenged by both political demands and attitudes of the society at large. In trying to reconcile personal ethics with that of the organization, Army officers face a dilemma (Snider, Nagl, and

---

[5]According to Snider et al., the three components of military professionalism are military-technical, ethical, and political.

Pfaff 1999, 8). The beliefs of egoism and post-modern relativism can be held by regular Americans, "but they cannot be held by Army officers, the professional military ethic is not a relative ethic" (Snider, Nagl, and Pfaff 1999, 9). Snider et al. states that "the obligation to uphold it or any of its tenets does not arise because those in the profession said so, but rather because it is necessary if the profession is to be effective in its purpose of warfigthing" (1999, 9).

In *Dereliction of Duty: Johnson, McNamara, the Joint Chiefs of Staff, and the Lies that Led to Vietnam* published in 1998 Colonel H. R. McMaster chronicles the failures of U.S. leaders in charge of the Vietnam War and the impact of pursuing wrong strategies. Colonel McMaster's work illuminates the inner working of the political establishment and the rift between military leaders and civilian policy makers. Although, Colonel McMaster finds fault in all major players of the war, he is extremely poignant with his criticism of military leaders, particularly, the members of the JCS. Colonel McMaster described the members of the JCS as "five silent men," because in effect, they stood silently, even though they disagreed with how the war was going, and became compliant figures to the Johnson administration (McMaster 1998, 330). Colonel McMaster's work illustrates the complex relationship between military leaders and civilian policy makers, but most importantly, the catastrophic result of pursuing wrong strategies and flawed policies.

Voluminous contemporary writings about ethics in civil-military relations cover a wide range of themes on the subject. The writing on ethics in civil-military relations, as the literature review above, illustrates the complex issues which govern the subject. There are differing viewpoints on how to interpret actions by military professionals in the

23

context of how they made decisions and the actions they took. The literature offers context for reviewing actions to arrive at a conclusion on the validity of actions taken by military professionals. This chapter provided the available literature for this study. The review provides enough material to answer all research questions. The next chapter discusses the research methodology.

CHAPTER 3

RESEARCH METHODOLOGY

> The military profession exists to serve the state. To render the highest possible service the entire profession and the military force which it leads must be constituted as an effective instrument of state policy. Since political direction comes from the top, this means that the profession has to be organized into a hierarchy of obedience. For the profession to perform its function, each level within it must be able to command the instantaneous and loyal obedience of subordinate levels. Without these relationships, military professionalism is impossible. Consequently, loyalty and obedience are the highest military virtues.
> — Samuel Huntington, *The Soldier and the State*

This chapter explains the origin, foundation, and source of the methodology used in this study to provide the reader with a frame of reference and proper context for understanding the study. The intent is for the reader to comprehend the ethical decision making framework used and to aid in the understanding of relevant facts, issues, and data utilized in the study. To answer the primary and secondary research questions, this study uses a theoretical civil-military ethical decision making framework (civ-mil EDMF). The civ-mil EDMF is based on the work of Dr. Don M. Snider's "Dissent and Strategic Leadership of the Military Profession" and Navy Chaplain (Captain) George M. Clifford III from Dr. Martin L. Cook's work "Revolt of the Generals: A Case Study in Professional Ethics." Dr. Snider employs five factors for evaluation of the trust relationships: (1) gravity of issue, (2) relevance to expertise, (3) degree of sacrifice, (4) timing of dissent, and (5) authenticity as leader (Snider 2009, 20). Chaplain Clifford uses four categories of issues which might raise the dissent issue in increasing levels of severity: (1) an assigned responsibility the officer can perform with minimal moral discomfort; (2) an assigned responsibility the officer can perform only with substantial moral discomfort; (3) an assigned responsibility the officer can perform only at the cost of significantly compromising his or her moral standards; and (4) an assigned responsibility the officer cannot perform (Cook 2008, 10-11). Merging the key elements of the five factors for evaluating trust relationships and four categories of issues which raise dissent in increasing levels of severity resulted in the formulation of the theoretical civ-mil EDMF.

The theoretical civ-mil EDMF (see below) used in this study consists of the following factors: (1) policy issue–the main issue causing civil-military tension in a strategic context; (2) context of dissent–based on the level of expertise of military professionals coupled with the ethical dilemma driving the wedge between civilian policy makers and military professionals; (3) appropriate venue for discourse–analysis of the venue used by military professionals to express dissent; (4) proper course of action–this pertains to military professionals actions and available options; and (5) framework for compromise–the degree to which military professionals cannot perform or support a policy. The civ-mil EDMF allows for framing and answering the primary and secondary research questions in a proper context.

Table 1.   Civil-military Ethical Decision Making Framework

Factors of Civil-Military Ethical Decision Making Framework	President Truman vs. MacArthur	President Eisenhower vs. the Generals	The Generals Revolt
Policy issue			
Context of dissent			
Appropriate venue for discourse			
Proper course of action			
Framework for compromise			

Source: Created by author.

26

This study examines individual as well as group tensions between civilian policy makers and military professionals from different periods in U.S. history to determine if there are any similarities or unique circumstances which precipitate the tensions in civil-military relations and ethical dilemmas for military professionals. Using different events throughout U.S. history may allow for objectivity and better sampling. This chapter established how this study will answer the primary and secondary research questions using the civ-mil EDMF. Each of the case studies will be analyzed using the factors outlined in the civ-mil EDMF. It is not the intent of this study to pass judgment, rather to examine the actions and circumstances in order to provide a context for evaluating and determining the viability of the actions taken based on the civ-mil EDMF developed in this study.

CHAPTER 4

ANALYSIS

The U.S. military has a long tradition of strong partnership between the civilian leadership of the Department of Defense and the uniformed services. Both have long benefited from a relationship in which the civilian leadership exercises control with the advantage of fully candid professional advice, and the military serves loyally with the understanding that its advice has been heard and valued. That tradition has been frayed, and civil-military relations need to be repaired.
— Lee Hamilton and James Baker, *Iraq Study Group Report*

The previous chapter established the framework for how the study will answer the primary and secondary research questions. This chapter will answer the primary and secondary research questions using relevant data gathered from the previous chapters. The analysis of the case studies is preceded by a historical background which provides the context for the case studies. This allows for illuminating the issues relating to ethical dilemmas faced by military professionals. The goal is to provide context for the dilemmas faced to attain a better perspective on the actions taken by military professionals. It is important to provide the framework for the actions taken, because it directly impacts the understanding of the situation, and provides a basis for interpretation that would otherwise not be achieved if readers are not familiar with the case studies used in this study. It is critical that readers must first understand the environment which shaped the events to enable them to gain a better understanding of the whole situation that precipitated the events.

President Truman versus General MacArthur

The backdrop for President Truman versus General MacArthur was the Korean War, one of the most momentous events in the twentieth century. It essentially began in

June 1950, but its roots extend back to the Japanese takeover of Korea in 1910 and the partition of the Peninsula at the end of World War II (Tucker 2010, 421). The Korean War was both the first shooting war of the Cold War under the auspices of the United Nations and the first limited war of the nuclear age between the United States and China; it was the only time since World War II that two major powers met on the battlefield (Gurtov 2010, 2; Tucker 2010, 421). It has been largely described as the "forgotten war" in the United States for varying reasons, but it remains an enduring war for both North and South Koreans. For the United States, the Korean War became a test of credibility and resolve in the face of communist expansion in Southeast Asia (Gurtov 2010, 1). The conflict in Korea left an indelible mark. It institutionalized the security environment of the Cold War; militarized U.S. foreign policy; solidified the role of the United States as the "world's policeman;" and strengthened the relationship between European allies and North Atlantic Treaty Organization members (Tucker 2010, 431; Gurtov 2010, 2).

The Korean War also featured one of the most significant and high profile tensions in civil-military relations in the United States. Sitting U.S. President Truman had a very public confrontation with General MacArthur, the Commander in Chief Far East Command and Commander of United Nations Forces in Korea over the proper course of action in conducting the Korean War. President Truman sought to implement a limited war strategy in Korea to prevent further escalation of the conflict for fear that it could lead to a wider regional conflict or trigger World War III (Rovere and Schlesinger 1992, 239; Department of the Army 1950). President Truman's administration feared that escalating the conflict with China would elicit a response from the Soviet Union and heighten the conflict into World War III. General MacArthur viewed the Truman administration's limited war and containment policy as appeasement and advocated for a more robust response by delivering a decisive blow that would collapse the communist regime in China (Pearlman 2008, 36). General MacArthur sought to establish naval blockade of China, bombing of Manchuria, use of local dissidents from Taiwan, along with United Nations Forces in Korea to achieve his objectives (Tucker 2010, 429; Potter 1972, 137; U.S. Congress 1951). President Truman together with his key advisers believed at the time that use of nuclear weapons and local dissidents would not lead to a peaceful resolution; rather, it could inflame the situation and lead to a confrontation with the Soviet Union (Pearlman 2008, 136; Danner 1993, 5; Memorandum of Conversation 1951). General MacArthur failed to secure consensus and approval for his stated strategy to achieve total victory in Korea. To this end, he decided to air his grievance and policy disagreement with President Truman through media outlets and political supporters in Congress (Potter 1972, 116-117; Memorandum of Conversation 1951; Letter to Representative Martin 1951).

The major policy issue that drove the wedge between President Truman and General MacArthur was over the foreign policy strategy employed during the Korean War. President Truman along with his cabinet and military advisers believed containing the situation in Korea and preventing further escalation was the best option for the United States (Rovere and Schlesinger 1992, 62; Executive Secretary 1950).[6] Keeping the Korean War as a small regional conflict was critical to the success of the U.S. strategy. President Truman did not believe escalating the conflict was the right option for the

---

[6]Then Secretary of Defense George C. Marshall, Secretary of State Dean Acheson, and Chairman of the JCS General Omar Bradley all concurred with the limited war policy strategy in Korea.

United States because he did not want the country to be entangled into a wider conflict. Limiting the conflict was the best way to ensure the United States did not get mired in a war that was widely becoming unpopular at home. The policy of containment and limited conflict with China was meant to avert a response from the Soviet Union in order to prevent the conflict from becoming a global confrontation (Pearlman 2008, 268; Army Department Message 1950).

General MacArthur, on the other hand, saw the Truman administration foreign policy of limited war as a sign of weakness and sought to resolve the conflict by using all available means (Pearlman 2008, 329). At first, he believed the Chinese would not enter the conflict, but once they did, he thought the best option was to deliver a decisive blow to cause the collapse of the communist regime in China (Potter 1972, 137). General MacArthur deemed the current strategic policy in Korea would only lengthen the conflict and involve the United States in a protracted war. General MacArthur professed that the use of all available means would lead to a quick and decisive victory for the United States and United Nations Forces (Pearlman 2008, 329). His strategic view was strictly military; it lacked the political component under which President Truman was operating.

General MacArthur's context of dissent to the Truman administration's security policy objectives appears to come from both his long experience in the region and military expertise. General MacArthur believed escalating the conflict was the right solution because it would resolve all the underlying issues (Tucker 2010, 429). General MacArthur assumed defeating the Chinese would also deal a deadly blow to the global ambition of the Soviet Union to spread communism. General MacArthur was of the opinion that by escalating the conflict, he would be able to prosecute the war to a more conclusive and final outcome (Pearlman 2008, 100). In his best military judgment, he believed the solution was causing the collapse of the communist regime in China, which in effect also curtailed the global aspirations of communist expansion by the Soviet Union. By conducting aerial and naval bombardment of China, establishing a naval blockade, and using local dissidents from Taiwan, combined with United Nations forces he could cause the collapse of the Communist regime in China (Pearlman 2008, 270; Potter 1972, 137). General MacArthur's context of dissent is not without merit, but it comes from a purely military standpoint, devoid of political and social constraints. The ethical dilemma for General MacArthur was whether he could follow President Truman's foreign policy objective (which was contrary to his military thinking) or continue to argue his case until he achieved consensus or support for his plan.

General MacArthur chose to argue his views through media outlets and supporters in Congress (Potter 1972, 167; Press Release 1951). By making public statements about policy disagreement, General MacArthur undermined President Truman in showing partisan support to republican members in Congress. This is clearly not the best way to argue one's point of view or to articulate one's opinions about U.S. national strategy. Given the military chain of command, executive, and legislative channels, the proper venue for discourse would be to utilize these channels. General MacArthur had many options available to him to communicate his points of view on the conflict. Even with his long and storied career, he was still fallible and subject to the proper rules of military conduct. Voicing his opposition through media channels and proxies was not only inappropriate, but also improper because it removed objectivity in the process (Danner 1993, 23). By arguing his case through surrogates, the process of thorough discourse and examination was undermined. Instead of debating logical arguments, scoring political points drove the process (Potter 1972, 190). No good can come from the process when it is undermined by political partisanship because the outcome is based on political expediency. The appropriate debate and deliberations of U.S. strategic objectives can only be reached by factual, systematic, and reasoned debate.

The proper course of action would have been for General MacArthur to articulate his case through the proper channels within the U.S. government and military chain of command. This is critical for objectivity as illustrated above. Given his long tenure in the military, not only as a military leader but as a statesman, it is difficult to imagine why General MacArthur chose to argue his points of view through media outlets and surrogates. With his vast experience and knowledge, it is hard to imagine why he was so careless and ill-tempered with his actions. Resolving his grievance could have been handled more professionally by going through the proper channels. As Commander in Chief Far East Command and Commander of United Nations Forces in Korea, he certainly could have aired his reservations to President Truman himself (Potter 1972, 191). Failing in the option to secure buy-in from members of the chain of command and President Truman, he could have relinquished his command voluntarily. Military professionalism implies the requirement for voicing opinions and arguing points in an open and deliberate manner because this process allows for objectivity and reaching consensus (Danner 1993, 23). Using proxies to argue and speak on ones behalf is not only ineffective but shows lack of moral courage and inability to subject one's opinions through careful deliberation and rational debate.

Had they both been willing to see the available options, the framework for compromise between President Truman and General MacArthur could have led to a more amicable and deliberate examination of both points of view. Clear indications are that both men could have found a way to resolve their issues had they been more willing to find commonality in resolving their strategic differences. But, their personalities and temperaments got the best of them and resulted in the milieu that is considered to be one of the most egregious episodes in U.S. civil-military relations. Both individuals chose the path of enmity and least resistance instead of trying to find a compromise. General MacArthur could have found a way to execute the strategic policy of the Truman administration even with some reservations. But, his open adversarial dissent and failure to follow orders led to his removal. Failure to secure consensus or approval for his tactical plan, General MacArthur could have chosen a better path to express his dissatisfactions or military dissent.

General MacArthur could have done a lot more to resolve the issues which prompted his policy disagreement with President Truman. Even minor efforts on his part to "agree to disagree" with President Truman may have contributed greatly towards alleviating the tension and coming to a more tenable position (Danner 1993, 5). It is clear that General MacArthur faced an ethical dilemma between following orders against his best military judgment. A myriad of ways were more appropriate than his documented actions which led to his relief as Commander in Chief Far East Command and Commander of United Nations Forces in Korea. The position taken by President Truman at the time has been validated by history as the right course of action. General

MacArthur's actions still reverberate today with negative connotations and a stain on his otherwise storied military career.

President Eisenhower versus the Generals

The setting for President Eisenhower versus the Generals was post World War II and the dawn of the Cold War period. Following the end of World War II, the United States began a massive demobilization of its military personnel. Commencing with the Truman administration, defense spending was curtailed because of the prevailing thought among civilian policy makers that America's nuclear capability was enough to deter any potential adversaries (Bacevich 1986, 307). This line of thinking continued when President Eisenhower took office. Under a novel strategic policy called New Look, the United States sought to leverage U.S. economic capacity and nuclear weapons as deterrents against the Soviet Union and other potential adversaries instead of a huge conventional military force (Executive Secretary 1953). The New Look policy purposely sought to create deep cuts in defense budgets and military personnel end strength, particularly, in the U.S. Army which precipitated the disagreement between U.S. Army senior leaders and the Eisenhower administration. The plan was viewed by senior Army officers particularly Generals Matthew B. Ridgeway and his subsequent replacement Maxwell D. Taylor as a grave threat to the very existence of the U.S. Army because it prevented the Army from performing its core missions (Bacevich 1997, 312).

This disagreement created a rift between the President and his senior Army leaders resulting in fundamental changes to the structure of the military chain of command, particularly the JCS with the passage of Defense Reorganization Act of 1958 (Cole et al. 1978, 188-230). President Eisenhower brought with him to the oval office a great deal of military expertise. His view on reduction of forces and defense spending cuts came from his inside knowledge of the system and what he believed needed to be done (Bacevich 1997, 307). The Generals viewed their dissent as trying to save their institution, a clear demarcation from what President Eisenhower wanted in terms of policy. They believed maintaining high force level structure was essential in meeting and performing U.S. Army missions (Taylor 1972, 23).

The main focal point of the policy issue disagreement that brought about the discord between President Eisenhower and Generals Ridgeway and Taylor centered on President Eisenhower's New Look national strategic security policy. The New Look policy proposed to use U.S. economic capacity and nuclear weapons instead of a standing conventional military to deter the Soviet Union and other potential adversaries around the world (Executive Secretary 1953). The principle tenet of the New Look policy was the threat of massive retaliation against the Soviet Union using nuclear weapons in the event of unavoidable confrontation between the two nations (Craig 1998, 52). The New Look policy aimed to dramatically slash defense spending (at its height the Army's budget fell from 32.1 to 25 percent) and manpower (Army personnel reduction target was 300,000) to curtail runaway government spending, in order to stabilize the U.S. economy (Condit et al. 1992, 238-239). The New Look policy sought to use and leverage the U.S. economy as a weapon to thwart the Soviet Union's aspirations of global expansion.

Under the new plan, the Army faced significant cuts in manpower and budget allotment which threatened the ability to perform its mission. The Army Chief of Staff at that time, General Matthew Ridgeway, voiced his disagreement not with the policy itself, but on the shortfalls to the Army's budget and manpower plans (Carter 2007, 363).

General Ridgeway believed the cuts did not pass or merit the justification because the Army's force commitments were not reduced. Even with the cuts, the Army would still perform its commitments around the world. The cuts also threatened the Army's ability to conduct both conventional and limited conflict capability, because it would not be able to maintain the required end strength and fund the acquisition of necessary equipment (Craig 1998, 75).

The context of dissent for General Matthew Ridgeway and his successor General Maxwell Taylor revolved around three factors. First, the belief that the proposed cuts to the Army threatened its existence and ability to perform its core mission; personnel and spending cuts would leave the Army with the same commitments but unable to fulfill or perform these commitments (Carter 2007, 367; Taylor 1956, 6-7). Second, their dissent was based on what they believed to be flaws in the massive retaliation doctrine of the New Look policy; Generals Ridgeway and Taylor did not believe confrontation with the Soviet Union would lead to a nuclear exchange. The likely threat was a limited conflict or engagement through a third party (Craig 1998, 47). The Generals did not necessarily disagree with President Eisenhower's new policy, but they were expressing views from the perspective of their service component. The Generals were not making any social, political, or economic calculations in their thinking which they believed was not in their purview. Third, the crux of the issue was President Eisenhower's demand that the Army, along with the other services, support his plan without any reservations (Carter 2007, 368). The Generals tried to engage the President in a discussion to help him see their points of view. Instead of engaging them in a discussion, he viewed their dissents as personal attacks and disloyalty. The ethical dilemma for the Generals was whether to blindly acquiesce to the President's demands when they did not agree with his strategic policy.

For the most part, the Generals used the proper command channels available to them. Only later, after their retirement did they use other mediums to express their disagreement with President Eisenhower. They did not go outside the proper mainstream channels to express their views. When asked for their opinions by Department of Defense officials, Congress, or the President on the new plan and proposed budget cuts they replied without equivocation of what they believed was their best military answer (Carter 2007, 365). The Generals expressed their disagreement with the basic premise of massive retaliation because of recent Soviet Union progress in science and technology relating to nuclear capability. They predicted that the looming force reduction and budgetary cuts would impact the Army's ability to perform its mission (Ridgeway Testimony 1956). The Generals expressed their views on the New Look policy and the emerging or likely threat of the future (Taylor 1959, 28; Ridgeway 1956, 269-273). The Generals' outlook was based on their military judgment and perception of future threats. They used the proper venues for discourse and were willing to debate their positions in an objective and factual manner.

In evaluating the proper course of action, the Generals largely did all the right things by keeping faith in the process and following protocols. They did not seek to antagonize President Eisenhower privately or publicly (Carter 2007, 365). They were very much aware of their roles, duties, and responsibilities. They exercised great restraint and moral courage in speaking their mind. They provided what they believed was their best military advice. They knowingly expressed their views with the full knowledge of

38

the personal repercussion of their actions. President Eisenhower could have done more to alleviate the situation but chose to ignore the situation by isolating himself from the service chiefs (Bacevich 1997, 330). The incident brought about the demise of the access and direct link by service chiefs to their Commander in Chief. This deprived them and the President of the opportunity for direct conversations. Now, the President and service chiefs have to go through bureaucratic channels to gain access to each other.

The framework for compromise was a bit muddled by the internal division within the Department of Defense and inter-service rivalry (Carter 2007, 357).[7] There was room for compromise, but the failure is mostly attributed to President Eisenhower, because he chose not to engage his former subordinates into a dialogue (Taylor 1972, 171). Rather, he viewed their dissent as personal attack and disloyalty against him. The Generals tried to work within the framework of the system in articulating their dissenting opinions. Their views, although not entirely incorrect were based on their analysis without the constraints of political and economic considerations under which the President was operating. Still, there was room for compromise on both sides had the President been willing to recognize the dissenting views of the Army. Personality and temperament played an important role in deciding the final outcome of the strategic disagreement. The President came into office with a great deal of military expertise and personal experience dealing with strategic military policies, which perhaps blindsided him from seeing the other perspective on military issues.

---

[7]Secretary of State John F. Dulles, Secretary of Defense Charles E. Wilson, and Chairman of the JCS General Nathan F. Twining supported the New Look policy but members of the JCS lobbied for their services.

Analysis of this case study reveals the stark contrast with President Truman versus General MacArthur's case study. This is because the Generals operated within the confines of the environment and system they were involved. When faced with an ethical dilemma, their actions reflected the proper course to take. They confronted the ethical dilemma with resounding success because they had a good understanding of their proper roles, duties, and responsibilities. They did not shirk from their responsibility. They embraced the challenge with an open mind by seeking consensus and resolution to the underlying issues (Carter 2007, 367). History would prove that both President Eisenhower and the Generals were correct in their positions. It is clear that the discord between President Eisenhower and the Generals created a rift, but it did not go in the way that General MacArthur and President Truman did. The case study implies that maintaining a proper balance between professional conduct and service requirements is critical to the success of military professionals.

The Generals' Revolt of 2006

The stage for the Generals' Revolt of 2006 was the Iraq War or Operation Iraqi Freedom, the operational name given and used by the U.S. military. By 2006, the Iraq War was not going well. It was in a tipping point due to sectarian violence and numerous miscalculations on the part of both military and civilian policy makers prompting an all out civil war in Iraq (Ricks 2007, 3-4). Four retired U.S. Army Generals, Major General Paul D. Eaton, Major General John R.S. Batiste, Major General John M. Riggs, and Major General Charles J. Swannack (and two U.S. Marine Generals) called for the ouster of then Secretary of Defense Donald Rumsfeld for his perceived negligence and mismanagement of the war in Iraq (Snider 2008, 4). The Generals believed Secretary

Rumsfeld was a divisive figure in the Department of Defense and the cause of many failures in Iraq. After retiring, the Generals argued for his relief publicly. This proved to be one of the main driving forces behind Secretary Rumsfeld's departure from the Pentagon.

The episode is unprecedented because the protagonists were retired military personnel purportedly speaking on behalf of their former colleagues in uniform (Owens 2007, 70). The dissent seemed to come not from within, but from without the normal channels of the chain of command. Although dissent of former military personnel was not new, the perception that retired military personnel are speaking for those who still wear the uniform was (Snider 2008, 3-4). This phenomenon had strategic impact with far reaching consequences. If retired military personnel spoke for former colleagues in uniform, it changed the dynamics of proper military channels. It also provided retired military personnel with enormous power to influence national strategic policy decisions. More importantly, this pointed to a broken system within the Department of Defense. Military professionals could not speak the truth to people in power for fear of reprisals from civilian heads or policy makers. The precursors to the Generals' Revolt of 2006 were the faulty information used to justify the invasion of Iraq, failures in planning, bad decisions made after completion of major combat operations, and retribution for dissenting opinions expressed by military professionals which ran counter to the Bush administration position (Snider 2008, 4; Rick 2007, 4; Woodward 2004, 193).

The central theme of the policy issue disagreement causing the rift in the Generals' Revolt of 2006 was the apparent mismanagement of the Iraq War by Secretary Rumsfeld. This was exacerbated by his failure to listen or accept the advice of military

41

commanders in charge of the war (Owens 2006, 71; Woodward 2004, 440). The main contention of the Generals was Secretary Rumsfeld becoming ineffective and losing the confidence of military professionals in the Defense of Department. Their argument was based on the deteriorating condition in Iraq, failure in planning, bad decisions, and lack of a coherent effort on how to turn the tide (Ricks 2007, 168-170; Owens 2006, 70-71; Woodward 2004, 193). What broke the proverbial camel's back according to the Generals was Secretary Rumsfeld's abrasive personality and continued insistence on completing the mission without proper resources to do it with (Snyder 2006, 1).

For his part Secretary Rumsfeld did not really try to address the policy issues raised by the Generals. He was dismissive regarding this when asked by reporters for his comment. He tried to pacify the growing clamor for his removal by ignoring it. Instead of reflecting on the issues being raised, he was rather quick to dismiss them (Snyder 2009, 4). He presented an outlook that while the war in Iraq was not currently going well, it was moving in the right direction, even though there was no clear path or strategy in place to mirror or support his optimism. Secretary Rumsfeld seemed to disregard the incongruence between events on the ground in Iraq and his optimistic outlook for the future (Snyder 2009, 4-5). It was perhaps callousness or extreme confidence that he could reverse the situation in Iraq that was displayed as he continued to perform his job.

The context of dissent by the retired Generals is that they spoke for their colleagues who were still in uniform. They appeared to express the sentiments of their former colleagues who were unable to express dissatisfaction and who disagree with the current direction of the Iraq War (Snider 2008, 3-4). The main context of their dissent was that Secretary Rumsfeld was too rigid, rude, and incompetent (because of the many

42

mistakes in Iraq) to continue to lead the Department of Defense (Ricks 2007, 169; Snyder 2009, 6). They back their assertions by highlighting the numerous failures in Iraq before, during, and after the invasion. Even though there were no coordinated efforts between the Generals in voicing their oppositions to Secretary Rumsfeld, the remarkably similar assertions echoes a unified position based on professional expertise and relevant experience (Snider 2008, 4). The Generals appeared to have been beset between speaking their minds while still in service and being perceived as disloyal to the Bush administration. The Generals' dissentions had the appearance that they were speaking for colleagues still in uniform.

The retired Generals' choice for venue to air their dissatisfaction was through media outlets via interviews and newspaper articles. There is no evidence to suggest a collective effort among the Generals for choosing to speak publicly. But, by making public their critique of Secretary Rumsfeld, they seemed to imply both contempt and admonition (Owens 2006, 4). There was no effort on their part to seek an audience with Secretary Rumsfeld or with President George W. Bush to voice their grievances privately. Advocating for change or arguing a position requires a deliberate process to determine the veracity of the case being advocated or argued. Without objectivity and purposeful deliberation of all the facts and options, it is impossible to arrive at a definitive outcome or plausible solutions (Cook 2008, 8). Working from within the system is perhaps the best course of action because it allows for testing the system itself. If coercion and acquiescence triumphs over deliberation and objective analysis, the system in place is clearly defective and in need of serious overhaul or replacement.

Without due process in formulating strategy, it is impossible to formulate strategic policy that will be effective in achieving desired end states.

In searching for the proper course of action, it is clear that the lines of communications between Secretary Rumsfeld and the Generals were strained beyond repair. This being the case, there is little if any venue to really try to resolve the issues. Perhaps, the proper course of action still would have been private conversations between Secretary Rumsfeld and the Generals. Being retired, they did have the option to speak their minds freely; former soldiers deserve the right to be heard especially dealing with military matters related to their training and experience. The Generals after all have earned the right to speak and be heard in those matters.

It is hard to determine what the proper course of action is here because the retired Generals were speaking as private citizens; as such they have every right to voice their opinions.[8] But, if they were speaking on behalf of their former colleagues, there should have been a measure of protocol in their actions. Reaching out to the Secretary of Defense or the President of the United States for that matter for a private audience should have been undertaken at a minimum. In the end their public and outspoken criticism was tainted as political because their actions reflected a coordinated attacked towards Secretary Rumsfeld and his relief (Owens 2006, 76). Their actions seemed to be motivated by personal vendetta and not representative of what they purported it to be.

The framework for compromise here may not be applicable because the Generals are no longer part of the institutions they purport to represent. Because of this, they do

---

[8]Retired generals are still subject to the Uniform Code of Military Justice even though they are no longer on active duty service.

not have a stake in the final outcome beyond that of personal satisfaction. The framework for compromise in this case study is marginally important because any changes that were made on behalf of their action did not impact them directly. There was also the question of do they really represent their former colleagues or not? Arguing the case for or against is not within the purview of this study.

The notion that the retired Generals were speaking on behalf of their former comrades is disconcerting. If those who are still in uniform cannot express their dissatisfaction on their own resolve, there is a wider and deeper issue within the U.S. Army. This implies that we have military professionals who are acquiescent in order to keep the status quo and reluctant to buck the system for fear of retribution. This might be a greater issue than the actions of the former Generals. If military professionals cannot speak their mind freely because of retribution, the system fails, because part of the job of military professionals is to speak the truth to people in power even at the cost of personal hazard (Ricks 2012, 27).

This chapter analyzed the case studies using the civ-mil EDMF to answer the primary and secondary research questions. It illustrated the different scenarios, contrasting level of responsibility, and type of situations where tensions could occur between military professionals and civilian policy makers in pursuing strategic objectives. The next chapter presents the conclusions and recommendations of this study based on the analysis of the case studies and pertinent information gleaned during the course of this study.

CHAPTER 5

CONCLUSIONS AND RECOMMENDATIONS

> Personal and professional honor do not require request for reassignment or retirement if civilians order one's service, command, or unit to act in some manner an officer finds distasteful, disastrous, or even immoral. The military's job is to advise and then execute lawful orders. . . . If officers at various levels measure policies, decisions, orders, and operations against personal moral and ethical systems, and act thereon, the good order and discipline of the military would collapse.
>
> — Richard H. Kohn, *Huntington's Challenge*

Chapter 5 presents the conclusions derived from the analysis of the case studies and lays out recommendations aimed at addressing the dilemmas identified. The purpose is to present plausible solutions that could help enhance civil-military relations. The objective is that by highlighting the issues, this will lead to the development of a contemporary theory or model to address modern civil-military relations friction points. The formulation of a contemporary and comprehensive civil-military relation theory which includes the different factors that impact civil-military relations is critical to finding resolutions to the issues identified in this study. Although, the civ-mil EDMF proved effective in providing context for understanding the ethical dilemmas faced by military professionals, it does not provide the final solution for resolving ethical dilemmas; this remains elusive. The civ-mil EDMF does provide guidelines from which to draw that could help members of the civil-military relation spectrum in trying to resolve disagreement or find solutions to issues confronting them.

Conclusions

In President Truman versus General MacArthur, this study concludes that the policy issue taken by President Truman during the Korean War was effective in preventing the regional conflict from becoming a wider confrontation that could have engulfed not just the region but the rest of the world (Rovere and Schlesinger 1992, 239). The context of dissent taken by General MacArthur would prove incorrect. The policy of limited war advocated by the Truman administration worked in containing the conflict, but led the United States on a path that would lead to another conflict not very different from the Korean conflict in Vietnam. The appropriate venue for discourse was within the military chain of command and U.S. government executive and legislative channels. Upon retirement General MacArthur continued to argue his case, but it fell on deaf ears as his positions became indefensible given the changes in the operational environment (Potter 1972, 191-192). The proper course of action for General MacArthur to prevent his ouster was reconsidering his positions and following specific orders given to him (Memorandum of Conversation 1951). His ill-tempered attitude contributed greatly to his own undoing. The framework for compromise was maintaining the supremacy of civilian control over the military. Civilian supremacy over the military must never be put into question.

The decision to go to war and how it is to be conducted will inevitably test and produce tensions between civilian policy makers and military professionals. It is important that all parties of the civil-military dialogue understand the decision to go to war and its conduct requires collaboration among them to be effective and successful (Connelly 2010, 29). Ultimately, they are responsible for designing and implementing the

47

plans and instruments used for the conduct of war and its successful conclusion. It is critical that both civilian policy makers and military professionals grasp the real significance and principle of effective civil-military relations. Civilian policy makers must understand that to employ both effective policy and strategy requires the use of proper military instruments (Bennett 2010, 2). Military professionals must maintain their voice in the formulation of strategy with a clear understanding of the role of politics in the conduct of war (Connelly 2010, 28). They must also accept civilian policy makers having a vote on the goals and how the war is conducted. Military professionals must maintain their ability to candidly voice their opinions throughout the policy and strategy decision making process.

In President Eisenhower versus the Generals, this study deems the policy positions taken by the President and the Generals that caused the dilemma proved to be correct with the passage of time. President Eisenhower's policies revitalized the U.S. economy, prevented a nuclear war, and defused confrontations with other countries. The Generals' dissent in maintaining faith and commitment to the utility of conventional forces and embrace of the limited war doctrine proved their worth in the subsequent decades (Carter 2007, 359). The appropriate venue for discourse was strained by President Eisenhower's refusal to consider the Generals' points of view. The disagreement created a lasting impact on how military policy is decided with President Eisenhower's reorganization of the Defense Department in 1953 and 1958. President Eisenhower's restructuring came as a response to the failure to achieve consensus among members of the JCS and reprisal over the disagreement with Army service chiefs. Because of these changes, service chiefs were detached from any direct advisory role when it came to designing military policies. Succeeding Presidents have had to work around bureaucratic red tape to attain broad, sound military counsel. The course of action taken by the Generals perhaps saved the Army from an institutional crisis. The framework for compromise illustrates the need to maintain the ability to speak the truth to people in power by military professionals.

Advice and opinions military professionals provide to civilian policy makers are critical in determining the ways and means that will accomplish the ends established by the civilian policy makers (Bennett 2010, 2). It is impossible to imagine why civilian policy makers will develop national security strategies for the Army to accomplish and not resource it with all the requirements to achieve them (Bennett 2010, 3). The best way for civilian policy makers to understand military capabilities and requirements is to listen to what military professionals have to say. Even with his depth of experience, President Eisenhower was shortsighted in his assessment of the emerging operational environment; he failed to see the emerging paradigm of limited war. Decisions to go to war are not made in a vacuum or by pure military ends. Subordinating the political dimensions of the policy to the military aspect is wrong because politics is the reason for going to war (Clausewitz 1976, 87). Military professionals must understand the social, political, and economic elements of policies established or created by civilian policy makers. These elements are the driving force providing the context for constraint and freedom of movement in the political realm. Failure to consider, analyze, and understand the social, political, and economic dimensions of policies results in tensions. Military professionals cannot be just one-dimensional in their outlook of things, particularly in understanding strategy and policies, because of their complexities. Strategies and policies have social, political, economic, and moral components (Bell 2013).

In the Generals' Revolt of 2006, this study finds that the protagonists positions causing the ethical dilemma did not fit within the civ-mil EDMF. Some of the factors did not apply to the main issues, but it is critical to note the impact of the actions by both sides. Secretary Rumsfeld's propensity to marginalize military professionals who possess an opposing view from his own positions may have contributed to the initial failures in Iraq (Snyder 2009, 7). By narrowing his pool of advice to those who agree with his line of thinking, objectivity in the process of designing strategies may have been limited or resulted in failing to consider all available options and outcomes. The politicization of military professionals will inherently have a negative effect on the profession of arms. Military professionals must remain outside the prey of politics. It is one thing to be politically astute, yet another to be politically partisan. Retired military professionals have the right to speak their minds. They are also entitled to any compensation when providing expert opinions as analysts. But what they are not allowed to do is to imply that they represent their former colleagues when they do not.

The study illustrates that there are varying degrees and dimensions causing tensions in civil-military relations. There are no universal issues or factors that automatically create tensions, but personality and temperament play critical roles in deciding the outcome of the tensions. No relationship can survive without conscious effort put into it by both parties (Bennett 2010, 2). One of the primary reasons determined by this study for the cause of frictions in civil-military relations is the civilian policy maker's propensity to ignore and marginalize military professionals and the counsel they provide when it goes against their viewpoint. Successful civil-military relationship requires partnership with each associate having his or her own part to play and responsibilities to uphold (Bennett 2010, 3). The military's role is codified in Goldwater-Nichols Act which requires it to inform the President, the Secretary of Defense, and the National Security Council with professional military advice and opinion. [9] The civilian role is undefined because there is no legal requirement for civilian policy makers to listen or hear advice, no matter how credible or reasoned it is (Bennett 2010, 30).

Albeit circumstantial, the final conclusion derived from the case studies is that limited experience in politics, lack of strategic depth, and gaps in professional education by military professionals impact the quality of civil-military relations. The three case studies analyzed illustrate that lack of political insight, strategic depth, and personality conflicts all contribute to the tensions and ethical dilemmas faced by military professionals. It is also essential to realize that U.S. civil-military relations do not merely entail civilian control of the military, because civilian control is already firmly established in the United States and is fully accepted without question by military professionals. The more important issue in U.S. civil-military relations is how to guarantee the effective use and employment of the military in pursuing national strategies (Bennett 2010, 31). To ensure this happens requires putting in place an integrated approach, deliberate system, a disciplined process, and constant dialogue between civilian policy makers and military professionals.

---

[9]The Goldwater-Nichols Department of Defense Reorganization Act of 1986 was enacted to facilitate jointness in the military and to fully define the roles of the military and civilian leadership.

Recommendations

The following recommendations are presented based on the analysis and conclusions made in this study. The majority of the recommendations were briefly discussed or slightly covered in the study because they were on the periphery of the core topic of this study. To this end, they require further study and analysis to determine their usefulness and impact towards enhancing civil-military relations.

This study was not able to examine the professional military education (PME) that military professionals undergo. It is worthwhile to study PME at great length to determine if there are any gaps in the process. Identifying the gaps may provide insight into how to best develop military professionals so they have a well-rounded education. Throughout the PME system there has to be a conscious effort made to educate military professionals more extensively on civil-military relations, Army ethics, and strategic studies. Perhaps, starting at the Command and General Staff College level is sufficient, but the Army should look into pushing to begin this at lower levels in an effort to build a more solid foundation and emphasis. A course in civil-military relations should examine theories and case studies like the ones used in this study to allow students to better understand the dynamics of civil-military relations. This is critical in building a framework for military professionals to think more deeply about factors that impact not only relations but also the development of strategic policies.

Ethics throughout the PME system are also important in broadening the ethical perspective and dimension of military professionals. There is no reason to believe that military professionals are lacking in ethics, however, discussion in this field of study will allow for better understanding of the principle tenets of Army ethics. Military

52

professionals will benefit from not only examining case studies and philosophies, but also internalizing and debating theories and events enabling them to trace the pitfalls. Thereby they will have the means to prevent them in the future. The Army is a values based institution; the more values and ethics are articulated and debated, the better it is for the institution because it allows for examination, reflection, and re-orientation. The more military professionals are immersed in ethical dilemmas, the better prepared they are to confront them. There is a big difference between doing the right thing tactically and ethically (Olsthoorn 2011, 3). Lapse in ethical judgment has far reaching consequences as the Abu Grab prison incident demonstrated in the Iraq War.[10]

Continued integration of other government agencies is vital. Through developmental PME, like the Command and General Staff College where they accept students from other U.S. agencies would facilitate becoming familiar with the Army's systems and processes. The interaction and exchange of ideas that happen between Army and interagency students help build relationships and understanding. This should be further enhanced to include higher and lower levels of the PME. Investing in education that allows for mutual benefit between the Army and other government agencies will not only ensure the skill to function in a joint environment, but will also build trust and the ability to relate and understand the Army culture by other government agencies. The Army as an institution also benefits from the experience of having interagency interaction because it facilitates better communication and understanding of other governmental agency's culture and processes.

---

[10]We are still perhaps living with the consequences of that infamous incident.

A core study in strategic policy formulation, design, and implementation will go a long way towards improving and providing military professionals the requisite knowledge needed to deal will strategic issues. The intent is not to make them experts in strategic design but simply able to understand the factors that influence strategic policies. Providing this experience enhances a deeper understanding of strategic decision making from a broader perspective. The limited view of operational level analysis is no longer sufficient, because the current operational environment requires a wider outlook. This can only be gained by making it mandatory through the PME process. Military professionals gain expertise at the tactical and operational level because of the emphasis placed on it in the PME. Emphasizing strategic level thinking will produce the same needed result.

Because less than 22 percent of members in Congress and only three cabinet members in the Obama administration have military background, there has to be a concerted effort by the Army to let government officials know who represents the Army (Manning 2012, 7). Although the Army has an on-going effort to brief new members of Congress, there is little interest being shown by new legislators (Raymond 2012). Because this is not mandatory, there is little the Army can do to force new members of Congress to attend. The Army must continue to devise means to reach out to government officials, because it is critical that government officials know who serves and how military professionals are trained and developed. This will enhance better understanding of how the Army works and who represents the Army. It may be uncertain how much this effort will impact relations and understanding of the Army by government officials, but it is a means to try to fill the gap between government officials and military professionals in the Army. Knowing how military professionals are trained and developed throughout their careers will allow government officials to understand not only their capabilities but also the culture and mindset inherent in the institution. Inviting newly appointed or elected civilian policy makers to Army PME institutions might be a good starting point.

This study highlighted the need for political experience by military professionals in order for them to gain the requisite know-how to deal with civilian policy makers at the strategic level. The Army currently provides a limited number of assignments to officers that provide political foundation. Conversely, very few officers have the opportunity to serve in congressional fellowships, office of the Secretary of Defense, or other governmental agencies (Bennett 2010, 28). The other issue is that only few actually seek these assignments, because current promotions are based on time with troops. Lack of troop command time is a disadvantage during the selection process. The current promotion system prefers to select tactical leaders for promotion to higher ranks. This system does not allow for preparing military professionals to operate effectively in a political environment. In order to better position military professionals and improve civil-military decision making process, the Army should develop a modified career or dual track that allows and promotes Army officers who delve into assignments in the political realm (Bennett 2010, 28).

The current political and security environment in the United States suggests the need to shift from the traditional theory in civil-military relations to one of a more contemporary model or integrated approach that accounts for the overlapping jurisdiction of linking ends, ways, and means necessary for strategic success. This calls for the necessity to establish a new model creating a decision-making process which encourages candid advice and rigorous exchange of views and insights among members of the civil-military spectrum. There has to be a process in place that allows for candid dialogue and intellectual exchange between military professionals and civilian policy makers that does not penalize the former. The development of a new model or concept must take into account not only the new political and security environment, but also must balance and weigh the specific contributions, functions, and responsibilities of the members of the civil-military relations spectrum. The current theories in civil-military relations discussed in this study lack coherence because of the gaps and flaws within the different theories. However, they provide context for understanding the issues and relationship by members of the civil-military spectrum. This perhaps, may be as good as it gets, when it comes to civil-military relations because of differences in opinions, preference, and methodology by different presidential administrations who assume the mantle of leadership.

The Army has many differing institutional values or creeds developed throughout the years. Some of these are written in military manuals, regulations, doctrine, or expressed in traditions. The Army should create a formalized professional ethic like other professions (e.g., Hippocratic Oath taken by physicians) that embodies its highest ideals and aspirations (Moten 2010, 20). It should inspire confidence and exemplify proper conduct for military professionals. Creating a single and all encompassing Army professional ethic will enable Army professionals to live by a standard common to all. This will negate confusion, uncertainty, vagueness, or unfamiliarity common among institutions that do not have a formal creed that guides their actions (Hartle 2004, 73-74). There is legitimate concern with formalizing a professional ethic, especially with litigation, but the Army could resolve this by creating a document that highlights the standards of the profession. This will allow its members to fully understand and articulate these ideals.

Military professionals must continue to maintain and enhance the trust relationship with the American population and civilian policy makers. Maintaining the hard won bond of trust with the American people must be an imperative that never wanes. Regardless of the state of the relationship with civilian policy makers, military professionals must maintain their professionalism, humility, and deference to civilian authority. The supremacy of civilian control over the military must never be put into question. Military professionals must understand that they do not have a monopoly on expertise in national security issues and strategies. They must expect civilian policy makers to challenge and engage them in dialogues to test their expert knowledge. Military professionals must continue to seek professional development where they see gaps in their education. Because there are no immediate solutions to some of the issues, gaps, and challenges identified in this study, military professional must endeavor in the meantime to develop individual contingency plans which address what is lacking in their professional development.

Sometimes, it is easy to forget the contributions made by our military professionals for political expediency. It is easy to overlook the lifetime commitment they made in the service of the nation to score political points. Military professionals are easy targets and prey sometimes, because they are expendables. When warranted by political expediency, it is easy to isolate, marginalize, or expel them. But, doing this for political expediency or to settle personal vendetta is bad for the country because it undermines the value of military service to the nation. Individuals who reach the rank of

57

general have invested their lives to a career of service. When they make a blunder, they have to be given a measure of compassion because they have dedicated their life to a calling that too few in the United States chose to undertake.[11] Military professionals should be punished if they commit a crime, but if they make a mistake or take actions based on their best military judgment; due consideration must be afforded them. Those who wear the uniform are willing to make the ultimate sacrifice, there has to be some value invested in that. Civilian policy makers do not have to listen or consent to military advice. But, they should use some measure of care when they make judgment or take actions against military professionals. The way military professionals are treated reflects how military service is valued by the nation and the American people.

---

[11]According to a survey conducted by the Department of Defense published on 28 November 2011, less than one percent of the American population has been on active duty service in the military.

REFERENCE LIST

Abbott, Andrew. 1988. *The system of professions: An essay on the division of expert labor*. Chicago, IL: University of Chicago Press.

Anderson, Fred, and Andrew Cayton. 2005. *The dominion of war: Empire and liberty in North America, 1500-2000.* New York: Penguin Group.

Avant, Deborah. 2004. The privatization of security and change in the control of force. *International Studies Perspectives* 5, no. 2: 153-157. http://psm.du.edu/media/documents/related_resources/avant_privatization_of_security_and_change_in_control_of_force.pdf (accessed 19 October 2012).

Bacevich, Andrew J. 1986. *The pentomic era. The US Army between Korea and Vietnam.* Washington, DC: National Defense University.

————. 1997. The paradox of professionalism: Eisenhower, Ridgway, and the challenge to civilian control, 1953-1955. *Journal of Military History* 61: 303-334. http://vi.uh.edu/pages/buzzmat/vnarticles/bacevichikeandridgway.pdf (accessed 12 October 2012).

Bell, Daniel M. 2013. Military ethics. Lecture, Eisenhower Auditorium, Fort Leavenworth, Kansas, 24 January.

Bennett, Douglas W. 2010. Military advice and civil-military relations. Monograph, School of Advance Military Studies, Ft Leavenworth, KS.

Bremer, L. Paul, and Malcolm McConnell. 2006. *My year in Iraq: The struggle to build a future of hope.* New York: Simon and Schuster.

Cahn, Steven M. 2002. *Classics of political and moral philosophy.* New York: Oxford University Press.

Carter, Donald Alan. 2007. Eisenhower versus the generals. In C100, Foundations, ed. Department of Joint, Interagency, and Multinational Operations, C161RB 357-376. Fort Leavenworth, KS: Government Printing Office, June.

Center for the Army Profession and Ethic (CAPE). 2012. *Americas Army–Our profession.* http://cape.army.mil/aaop/aaop%20overview/overview.php (accessed 17 November 2012).

Clausewitz, Carl von. 1976. *On War.* Edited and Translated by Michael Howard and Peter Peret. Princeton, NJ: Princeton University Press.

Coffman, Edward M. 2004. *The regulars: The American Army, 1898-1941.* Cambridge, MA: The Belknap Press of the Harvard University Press.

Cohen, Eliot. 2002. *Supreme command.* New York: Simon and Schuster.

Cole, Alice C., Alfred Goldberg, Samuel Tucker, and Rudolph Winnacker, eds. 1978. *The Department of Defense: Document on establishment and organization 1944-1978.* Washington, DC: Historical Office of the Office of the Secretary of Defense.

Connelly, Donald B. 2010. The unequal professional dialogue: American civil-military relations and the professional military ethic. Professional Military Ethics Symposium, US Army Command and General Staff College, Fort Leavenworth, KS, 15-17 November.

Cook, Martin L. 2008. Revolt of the generals: A case study in professional ethics. *Parameters* 38, no. 1 (Spring): 4-15. http://www.dtic.mil/dtic/tr/fulltext/u2/a485882.pdf (accessed 17 October 2012).

———. 2004. *The moral warrior.* Albany, NY: State University of New York Press.

Cosmas, Graham A. 1971. *An Army for empire: The United States Army in the Spanish-American War.* Shippensburg, PA: White Maine Publishing Company.

Craig, Campbell. 1998. *Destroying the village: Eisenhower and thermonuclear war.* New York: Columbia University Press.

Cunliffe, Marcus. 1968. *Soldiers and civilians: The martial spirit in America, 1775-1865.* Boston, MA: Little, Brown, and Company.

Danner, Stephen A. 1993. The Truman-Macarthur tug of war–a lingering aftermath? Master's Thesis, Air War College, Maxwell AFB, AL.

Dempsey, Jason K. 2009. *Our Army: Soldiers, politics, and American civil-military relations.* Princeton, NJ: Princeton University Press.

Department of the Army. 2012. Army Doctrine Reference Publication (ADRP) 6-22, *Army leadership.* Washington, DC: Government Printing Office.

———. 1950. Message, to Douglas MacArthur, 29 June. http://www.trumanlibrary.org/whistlestop/study_collections/koreanwar/index.php (accessed 18 April 2013).

Desch, Michael C. 2001. *Civilian control of the military: The changing security environment.* Baltimore, MD: Johns Hopkins University Press.

Duffy, Michael. 2006. The revolt of the generals. *Time Magazine*, 16 April. http://www.time.com/time/magazine/article/0,9171,1184048,00.html (accessed 15 October 2012).

Executive Secretary. 1953. Statement of policy by the National Security Council on the basic national security policy, NSC 162/2. http://www.fas.org/irp/offdocs/nsc-hst/nsc-162-2.pdf (accessed 12 April 2013).

———. 1950. Report to the National Security Council on U.S. courses of action in the event Soviet Forces enter Korean hostilities, 76/1. http://www.trumanlibrary.org/whistlestop/study_collections/korea/large/documents/pdfs/ki-16-4.pdf (accessed 12 April 2013).

Feaver, Peter D. 2003. *Armed servants: Agency, oversight, and civil-military relations.* Cambridge, MA: Harvard University Press.

Feaver, Peter D., and Richard H. Kohn. 2001. *Soldiers and civilians: The civil-military gap and American national security.* Cambridge, MA: MIT Press.

Finer, Samuel E. 1962. *The man on horseback: The role of the military in politics.* New York: Frederick A. Praeger.

Gaddis, John L. 1982. *Strategies of containment: a critical appraisal of American national security policy during the Cold War.* New York: Oxford University Press.

Gavin, James W. 1958. *War and peace in the space age.* New York: Harper.

Graham, Bradley. 2009. *By his own rules: The ambitions, successes, and ultimate failures of Donald Rumsfeld.* New York: Perseus Books Group.

Gray, Colin S. 2002. *Strategy for chaos: Revolutions in military affairs and the evidence of history.* Portland, OR: Frank Cass Publishers.

Gurtov, Mel. 2010. From Korea to Vietnam: The origins and mindset of postwar U.S. interventionism. *Asia-Pacific Journal: Japan Focus 42* (December): 421-433. http://lumen.cgsccarl.com/login?url=http://search.ebscohost.com/login.aspx?direct=true&db=poh&AN=54597622&site=ehost-live (accessed 13 February 2013).

Halper, Daniel. 2013. Obama fires top general without even a phone call. http://www.weeklystandard.com/blogs/obama-fires-top-general-without-even-phone- call_697744.html (accessed 12 March 2013).

Hamilton, Lee, and James Addison Baker. 2006. *Iraq study group report.* http://media.usip.org/reports/iraq_study_group_report.pdf (accessed 13 February 2013).

Hartle, Anthony E. 2004. *Moral issues in military decision making.* 2nd ed. Lawrence, KS: University Press of Kansas.

Herspring, Dale R. 2005. *The pentagon and the presidency: Civil-military relations from FDR to George W. Bush.* Lawrence, KS: University Press of Kansas.

Huntington, Samuel P. 1957. *The soldier and the state: The theory and politics of civil-military relations*. Cambridge, MA: Belknap Press.

Janowitz, Morris. 1960. *The professional soldier: A social and political portrait.* Glencoe, IL: The Free Press.

Joint Chiefs of Staff. 1951. Memorandum to Douglas MacArthur attached copy of letter from Douglas MacArthur to Joe Martin, 20 March. http://www.trumanlibrary.org/whistlestop/study_collections/koreanwar/index.php (accessed 18 April 2013).

———. 1950. Memorandum to Douglas MacArthur, 29 October. http://www.truman library.org/whistlestop/study_collections/koreanwar/index.ph (accessed 18 April 2013).

Kalb, Marvin, and Elie Abel. 1971. *Roots of involvement: The U.S. in Asia 1784-1971.* New York: W. W. Norton and Company.

Kohn, Richard H. 1994. Out of control: The crisis in civil-military relations. *The National Interest* 35: 3-17.

Korb, Lawrence J. 1976. *The Joint Chiefs of Staff.* Bloomington, IN: Indiana University Press.

Lee, Jeong. 2013. Firing a general for the sake of a feasible strategy. *Georgetown Journal of International Affairs.* http://journal.georgetown.edu/2013/02/06/firing-a-general-for-the-sake-of-a-feasible-strategy-by-jeong-lee/ (accessed 12 March 2013).

Letter to Representative Joe Martin 20 March 1951. http://www.trumanlibrary.org/whistlestop/study_collections/koreanwar/index.php (accessed 18 April 2013).

Mann, James. 2004. *Rise of the Vulcan's: The history of Bush's war cabinet.* New York: Viking Penguin.

Manning, Jennifer E. 2012. *Membership of the 112th Congress: A profile*. Washington, DC: Congressional Research Service.

Marshall, George C. 1945. The challenge of command; an address to the graduates of the first officer candidate school. In Selected Speeches and Statements of General of the Army George C. Marshall, Chief of Staff United States Army, ed. Harvey A. DeWeerd. *The Infantry Journal*: 220-221.

Matthews, Lloyd, J., and Don M. Snider, eds. 2005. *The future of the Army profession.* 2nd ed. Boston, MA: McGraw-Hill Custom Publishing.

Mattox, John, M. 2012. Military ethics. Lecture, Eisenhower Auditorium, Fort Leavenworth, KS, 13 September.

McMaster, H. R. 1998. *Dereliction of duty: Johnson, McNamara, the Joint Chiefs of Staff, and the lies that led to Vietnam.* New York: Harper Collins Publishers.

McNamara, Robert S. 1995. *In retrospect: The tragedy and lessons of Vietnam.* New York: Times Books.

Metz, Steven. 1993. *Eisenhower as strategist: The coherent use of military power in war and peace.* Carlisle Barracks, PA: Strategic Studies Institute. http://www.strategic studiesinstitute.army.mil/pdffiles/pub359.pdf (accessed 17 October 2012).

Miller, William I. 2000. *The mystery of courage.* Cambridge, MA: Harvard University Press.

Millett, Allan R., and Peter Maslowski. 1994. *For the common defense: A military history of the United States of America.* 2nd ed. New York: Free Press.

Moten, Matthew. 2010. The Army officers' professional ethic—past, present, and future. http://www.StrategicStudiesInstitute.army.mil/ (accessed 12 October 2012).

National Security Council Members. 1951. Memorandum of conversation. http://www.trumanlibrary.org/whistlestop/study_collections/koreanwar/index.php (accessed 15 April 2013).

Nielsen, Suzanne C., and Don M. Snider, eds. 2009. *American civil-military relations: the soldier and the state in a new era.* Baltimore, MD: Johns Hopkins University Press.

Office of the Historian. n.d. Foreign Relations of the United States, 1952-1954, Vol. 2, Part 1, National Security Affairs, Document 112. https://history.state.gov/ historicaldocuments/frus1952-54v02p1/d112 (accessed 12 April 2013).

———. Foreign Relations of the United States, 1952-1954, Vol. 2, Part 1, National Security Affairs, Document 107. http://history.state.gov/historicaldocuments/ frus1952-54v02p1/d107 (accessed 12 April 2013).

Olsthoorn, Peter. 2011. *Military ethics and virtues: an interdisciplinary approach for the 21st century.* New York: Routledge.

Owens, Mackubin T. 2006. Rumsfeld, the generals, and the state of U.S. civil-military relations. *Naval War College Review* 59, no. 4 (Autumn): 68-80. http://www.dtic.mil/cgi-bin/GetTRDoc?AD=ADA519804 (accessed 10 October 2012).

Pearlman, Michael D. 2008. *Truman and MacArthur policy, politics, and the hunger for honor and renown.* Bloomington, IN: University Press.

Potter, Allen R. 1972. The Truman-MacArthur controversy: A study in political-military relations. Master's Thesis, Command and General Staff College, Ft Leavenworth, KS.

Press Release. 1951. Speech of Representative Joseph W. Martin, 12 February. http://www.trumanlibrary.org/whistlestop/study_collections/koreanwar/index.php (accessed 18 April 2013).

Raymond, Col William. 2012. Thesis discussion. Eisenhower Auditorium, Fort Leavenworth, KS, 24 November.

Ricks, Thomas E. 2012. *The generals: American military command from World War II to today.* New York: Penguin Press.

———. 2006. *Fiasco: the American military adventure in Iraq.* New York: Penguin Press.

Ridgeway, Matthew B., and Harold H. Martin. 1956. *Soldier: The memoirs of Matthew Ridgeway.* New York: Harper Press.

Roman, Peter J., and David W. Tarr. 1998. The Joint Chiefs of Staff: From service parochialism to jointness. *Political Science Quarterly* 113, no. 1: 91-111. http://www.polisci.ufl.edu/usfpinstitute/2009/documents/readings/roman_tarr1998.pdf (accessed 12 October 2012).

Rovere, Richard H., and Arthur M. Schlesinger. 1992. *General MacArthur and President Truman: The struggle for control of American foreign policy.* New Brunswick, NJ: Transaction Publishers.

Schiff, Rebecca. 2009. *The military and domestic politics: A concordance theory of civil-military relations.* New York: Routledge.

———. 1995. Civil-military relations reconsidered: A theory of concordance. *Armed Forces and Society* 22, no. 1 (Fall 1995): 7-24. http://afs.sagepub.com/content/22/1/7 (accessed 12 October 2012).

Snider, Don M. 2008. Dissent and strategic leadership of the military professions. *Orbis* 52, no. 2: 256-277. http://www.dtic.mil/dtic/tr/fulltext/u2/a477064.pdf (accessed 15 October 2012).

Snider, Don M., and Gayle L. Watkins. 2000. The future of Army professionalism: A need for renewal and redefinition. *Parameters* 30, no. 3: 5-20. http://www.carlisle.army.mil/usawc/parameters/articles/00autumn/snider.htm (accessed 10 October 2012).

Snider, Don M., John A. Nagl, and Tony Pfaff. 1999. *Army professionalism, the military ethic, and officership in the 21st century.* Carlisle, PA: Strategic Studies Institute. http://www.dtic.mil/dtic/tr/fulltext/u2/a372493.pdf (accessed 15 October 2012).

Snyder, Lewis R. 2009. The generals' revolt and civil-military relations. Program Research Project, U.S. Army War College, CarlisleBarracks, PA.

Spanier, John W. 1959. *The Truman- MacArthur controversy and the Korean War.* Cambridge, MA: Belknap Press.

Taylor, Maxwell D. 1972. *Swords and plowshares.* New York: Da Capo Press.

———. 1960. *The uncertain trumpet.* New York: Harper and Brothers.

Tucker, Spencer C. 2010. The Korean War, 1950-53: From maneuver to stalemate. *Korean Journal of Defense Analysis* 22, no. 4: 421-433. http://lumen.cgsccarl. com/login?url=http://search.ebscohost.com/login.aspx?direct=true&db=poh&AN =54597622&site=ehost-live (accessed 13 February 2013).

U.S. Congress. House. 1956. Statement of General Maxwell Taylor before the Subcommittee on Department of Defense Appropriations of the Committee on Appropriations, House of Representatives Relative to the Department of the Army Budget for Fiscal Year 1957, 1 February.

———. 1955. Testimony of General Matthew B. Ridgeway, Chief of Staff, U.S. Army Before the Armed Services Committee, 31 January. Box 2, Chairman's Record. Admiral Radford, RG 218, NARA.

U.S. Congress. Senate. 1951.Committee on Armed Services and Committee on Foreign Relations. Compilation of Certain published information on the military Situation in the Far East, 82nd Cong., 1st-Sess.

Woodward, Bob. 2004. *Plan of attack.* New York: Simon and Schuster.

Yingling, Paul. 2007. A failure in generalship. *Armed Forces Journal* (May): 17-23. http://38south.com/docs/Defence/AFJMay2007.pdf (accessed 17 October 2012).